# One by One;
# Portraits of Mental Illnesses In America

## By
## Londa B.

Published by: Purposeful Publishing and Media Services
St. Louis, MO.
www.londab.com


One by One; Portraits of Mental Illness in America by Londa B.

**Cover Graphics by Londa B.**
**Artwork:** Frame 14 by Elementalimaging
Three Faces by Christos (Krisdog) Georghiou.
http://www.georghiou.supanet.com

This book is a work of non- fiction. The events described here, are all real. Chapter participants have requested to remain anonymous. The settings and characters names have been changed to protect the innocent. Any resemblance is entirely coincidental.

IBSN-13: 978-0-9831739-1-5
Library of Congress Control Number: On File

Printed in the United States of America


**2nd EDITION/PRINTING July 2016**

## ~Acknowledgements~

I would like to take this moment to thank my heavenly father. I thank him for the past, present and future. I thank him for rocking my soul to sleep on many restless nights. I thank him for waking me because there were times where I thought seeing daylight--- would only be in my dreams. Through all the trials and pains in life, I now understand my purpose. I have a newfound passion of helping others through sharing my experiences. There is nothing that can stop me, for I am strong, fearless and a child of God. I also want to take the time to thank my family. Chad, thank you for all you do. You are the true picture of dedication, faithfulness and strength. To my children...dream big and do big. Life waits on no one. To my mother, I love you with all of my heart. Through it all---, you have taught me to be the woman I am today! Thanks for all you have done dad, you mean the world to me. Thank you for speaking wisdom and knowledge into me. To my faithful readers, thank you for your continued support.

Many blessings

# ~Dedications~

I want to take the time to dedicate this book to individuals affected by mental illness. This dedication not only applies to those living with mental illness, but to the family members and service providers. I pray one day the world gathers enough courage and empathy to travel through your mental pathways to envision, as well as understand your struggles. The battle in the arena of mental health will be an ongoing battle, but victory is near as long as we stand together and make our voices heard. I pray this book changes how people view and feel about mental health issues.

I would also like to dedicate this book to my current physician, Dr. Radhika Rao and her wonderful staff. A special thank you goes to Dr. Kapal Datta! You answered that call in the early morning from a young woman looking for a way out of the darkness! You and God were working overtime that night! Last, but not least I would like to thank the individuals who opened their homes and their lives for this literary project. Your willingness to allow me to pen your lives will be a testimony to thousands around the globe!
Thank you!

# Other Books by Londa B.

*Who's Loving Me?*
*One Woman's Journey to Understanding what Self-Love and*
*Self-Preservation Means*

*My Soul Desires...*

*The Cougar Killer*

*Why Can't We Get It! Coming January 2017*

# ~Foreword~

What is mental illness? Is it something that deserves a special *hiding place* like last year's unwanted Christmas gifts? Is mental illness a Facebook tag you wish you were never associated with? Truth told... it's an issue that is no laughing matter.

Today, one in five Americans live with some form of a mental illness. If not diagnosed correctly, and treated; the results could be deadly. The task on raising awareness must take place. Every day on some platform of social media, we witness how individuals with mental illness make headlines for all the wrong reasons. It upsets me when I see people posting comments like, "This must stop, they're nuts, didn't someone see this coming, or it was just a matter of time..." on Facebook and then goes back to doing nothing. GET MAD! BE HEARD! DO SOMETHING!

If you do not know where to start, become a member of NAMI. NAMI is the National Alliance on Mental Illness. If you join and provide a small donation, you are doing something. NAMI is the leader of making voices heard as well as helping our country obtain reform in the arena of mental health. Please visit their website, there is an abundance of information on their website to help, inspire and educate the masses about mental health.

In life, we see many people on a daily basis who have some type of mental illness. But answer this, what about the silent sufferers? These are individuals who apply layers of *strong-face* as they wear their capes made for super heroes. African Americans are great at doing this. The reasoning of being a proud people; makes me uneasy. Even the strongest have moments of weakness. One cannot carry burden alone.

On January 11, 2008, the life I knew was re-arranged like living room furniture. I already knew that my clinical depression (earlier diagnosis) had me bound, gagged and ready for tossing into the trunk of *lost*. Feelings of hopelessness and severe rage presented its self on every channel except the news.

I decided to go see a doctor. After several test questions, surveys, and the examination of my family medical history; the dam broke. My ears were being flooded with words like, Bi-Polar, Post-Traumatic Stress Disorder, and Adult Attention Deficit Disorder.

"Yulonda...you are most definitely suffering from a variety of issues. The abuse you endured growing up is why you have PTSD." He stated in a sure-toned voice. Frozen with denial and stiffened with anger, embarrassment shadowed over me; and my soul ran off. He was also sure that the other underlying factor to my diagnosis was related to how mental illnesses ran rampant throughout my family tree.

The fear of being stereotyped as nuts, bipolar, or psycho induced me into a constant crying state. What will this new diagnosis mean? I reflected on my life, and in those few moments, I was calmed in knowing that the Lord doesn't make mistakes. Already heavily into researching on five mental illnesses to discuss in this book, here I stood as a newly diagnosed patient. You want to know something? One of the topics I researched ended up being my diagnosis. With that, I knew this book had to be brought forth. There was no question about it.

The person I'd chosen to be the portrait of one of my chapters, changed his mind and backed out the project. Well, guess who was left standing? You guessed right- me. A combination of my feelings being all over the place, and seeing myself embedded in the chapter titled: *BIPLOAR... NOW WHAT*, made me nervous. Was I ready to use my platform to share such personal news with the world? I thought to myself- well what would happen if I remained silent? How many people would know where to get help? I thought about my last talk with my father and he always said, "God has great use for you. Your purpose is right in front of you. *Lord, I accept this role... I think.*

After being on a roller coaster of emotions, I got off. I calmed down, and began a mental rewind of my past behaviors. Experiencing Manic episodes, crowning myself as the ruler of the world, extreme mood swings, issues with my brain never shutting off, poor communication skills, and issues with spending money; now had a name. I felt better knowing why I did the things I did.

I laughed at the A.D.H.D. diagnosis because I finally understood why I started a million projects in one day but never finished any. I understood how one minute I could be talking about what I was going to cook for dinner, to thinking about when I could fit the dog in with the groomer. Hell, once I thought I had super powers because I could look people dead in the face and not hear one single word. Even in writing, my first few literary projects were not as good as I desired them to be. I am so grateful for second editions.

On the next page, I had those moments where manic episodes created a beast. I worked for days straight, wrote and published books, cleaned my entire home all while attending to the needs of my family. This mess had to end.

The night I started taking my medications, my husband asked me what I want to do. There was no denying that not only did I owe it to myself, but I owed it to my family. Standing hand in hand, we stared at those six bottles of medication lined up on the dresser. I think he was more nervous than I was. He hugged me and took me into his arms and we prayed. We prayed for understanding, strength and the will to support one another no matter what. Quickly thereafter, he retrieved some water for me to down all those pills. We hoped a new and better version of me would appear.

What happened, you ask? In the beginning, the medicines had me loopy and close to landing the role for the new Rob Zombie; "Night of the Living Dead" movie. I was tired a lot and the medicine made me feel as if I was gliding on clouds. The world was abstract to me. You could have told me that my home burned down, my car was stolen, and told I was let go from my job all in one day, and I would have said, "That's nice." The medicines had me wondering who could float on clouds through such turbulent storms. Three and a half weeks later, peace and order began to surface.

Today, nothing gets to me as much. Mental health is manageable as long as you participate. I learned coping mechanisms on how to deal with life and its stressors. I also learn to stay away from trigger points. Please understand, even with giving one-hundred per-cent, I still have days here and there; but they are nothing like the past.

I invite you to take a tour of our galleries. Each person has a story to share. Again, I pray you will have some understanding as to what impact mental illness has on the society, the families, the care-takers, and those living with it. Recognizing a problem is the first step...acceptance and working things out is where the real work occurs.

*Londa B.*

One by One;
Portraits of Mental Illnesses
Gallery Contents

- Hyper-Sexually Speaking...
  I need Stimulation!
  ***Sexual Content***
  Jessica Davis

- Those Damn Voices Schizophrenia at
  its Worst... Daniel Adams with his
  mother, Betty.

- Bi-polar--- NOW WHAT?
  Author Londa B.

- My Depression Filled Life
  Rachael McDaniel

- Cut one...Cut two...Cut three,
  I Love Cutting!
  Megan Williams

One by One;
Portraits of
Mental Illness in
America.

At the end of this book, you will find a wealth of resources to help you or maybe a friend or loved one obtaining help. Please understand, not everyone needs medication. I do not want people to think the worse. Some people avoid getting help because they are afraid of doctor's, the health system, what the medicine might do to them, and last- what people may think of them. It's okay to get help.

Knowing you have a problem but choosing to do nothing about it doesn't help. Take a stand today. I pray you find your strength.

*"Never give up on someone with a mental illness. When "I" is replaced by "We", illness become wellness."*
-Shannon L. Alder

### *Hyper-Sexually* Speaking…
### I Need Stimulation!
### ***Sexual content***
### Jessica Davis

**"Although the world is full of suffering, it is full also of the overcoming of it."**
**-Helen Keller, *Optimism***

### ***WARNING SEXUAL CONTENT! ***

"Oh, come on now! Time after time, this man continuously runs late."

"Jess, please be patient! The doctor will be here in a few. We made a mistake and double booked a few people here and there, so there is a wait." The nervous nurse stuttered out as she shuffled through schedule book.

"You guys screw up a lot!" Jess bitched as she threw her iPhone into her purse.

"I promise, you are next to be seen!"

Waiting for what seemed to be forever, Jessica was adamant on telling her doctor on how today would be the last consult. Sold on her decision, Jessica practiced her speech on how she was going to announce her session to

the so-called doctor without a stethoscope!
*"One more session, no matter what he asks or thinks; I'm out of here. What a freak!"*

"Jessica, the doctor is ready to see you."

"Thanks for the wait, Shirley."

"Hello Jessica. Sorry I'm running late. I know Shirley made quite a mess with today's schedule; but we're back on track. I hope all is well with you. Let's start shall we?" Dr. Fitzgerald greeted Jessica with his intro script.

"Yes, let's get to it! I am done seeing you after today! This so-called therapy---" Jessica waved her hands in the air as her head bobbed from side to side, "and the down pouring of drugs you have been giving me is not working! Sex is on my brain, more than my damn skull! The constant need for releasing is out of control."

"I take it you have stopped taking your meds." He asks while jotting notes into that bullshit journal of his.

"Hell yeah, I have! I know I have an issue of wanting sex all the time, but damn, even when I try to have sex, I can't climax. My *stuff* needs to be defibrillated just to be brought back to life. You said it was going to pull the desire down, not bury it in a casket for life! Once I took myself off those meds, I got my feeling back. Sex was real again.

I could tell I pissed him off, he pulled up from his position of comfort as if he was about to tell me off.

I kept my stance, because he wasn't about to talk me out of what I wanted to do.

"Jessica, do you know what your behavior can do? Do you know how all of this will affect your husband when he finds out? Why haven't you told him? Do you like what you do?"

"Fuck off! Don't sit here and judge me you prick with all the degrees, plaques and picture perfect family. I guess the more degrees, awards, and letters of achievements you get; the more disconnected you become. I guess you do this to shield yourself from your own problems. "I hissed as I stared into Dr. Williams blue eyes.

"I'm not judging you. You are at a point to where something has to become of this, before major harm occurs. What would you do if you brought some type of STD? How could you live with the decisions you've made?

"I think you are missing the big picture here Doc. My mind has been fractured. Need I remind you? Let me tell you again. My ninth birthday was supposed to be special. My mother had planned it for months. But that lousy uncle of mine thought it was time to make me a *woman*. It went on for a while, and then suddenly…I wanted to lay him out, just as much as he wanted to spread me wide. He created something so ugly, so painful, so big---that I tried to kill myself five, count them; 1, 2, 3, 4, 5- times! I live, eat, and sleep with sex on my mind. THERE IS NEVER SATISFACTION! That night was hell awful and the scars have never left. Jessica was out of explanations.

"Please try to calm down. You were doing so well. We need to get you back on your meds." He was too calm. And I think his mind was in another place.

I acted before I could think; I stood up and charged Dr. Williams. He was going to listen to what I had to say. I knocked the journal out of his hand, took my hand, and forced his back well into the chair.

"Listen here Mr. Perfect! I have been telling you my stories of pain, rejection, shame, and depression for five years. What has it done for you? I know what these sessions do for me, but what do they do for you? Does helping me, give you thoughts of what it would be like to have a woman like me? A woman that's ready to screw at the sound of your zipper?" I straddled myself onto the doctor's lap.

"Hmm, it feels like that heart of yours is working over one-hundred beats per minute. You're displaying a case of tachycardia there doc- slow down. Why are you breathing so heavy? You are going to sit here and you are going to love how I lick in your ear, whisper warm and wet details on how I intend on turning you plain life into a circus. You need a woman like me. That's why you have kept me for five years. What man keeps a woman like me around for five years? Not one that wants conversation, I bet you that!"

"I---wait, we need to---. He stuttered as I decided to place my thick frame onto his hardened manhood.

"You have some secrets of your own and I know one of them. You are no better than me. *Your* addiction is *ME!* The last session we had, I left a pair of red lace panties on your bathroom sink. You left the room to answer an important call- which took way too long. So I figured, why not have a quickie? I *got* myself off real quick before you returned. Rushing, I simply forgot to place them in my handbag. That following week, I came back to see you. As usual, you ran late. While you left the room to grab me some new samples, something red and lacy caught my eye. I walked over and to my surprise; my panties were in your pocket! Did you think you could hide that from me?

"Please, don't tell." He begged as he looked away from me.

"Do you tell *your* therapist about me? I know you shrinks have to see someone for your own sanity. I ask because I question the effectiveness of your doctor.

Nothing flowed from his tight white lips. I continued to stare him down. I hope he had felt the same way I did on my ninth birthday.

"We share a lot. Like a druggie, we share the constant need for stimulation. My womanhood throbs and beats to different rhythm. The beats that come from within the walls of this tomb echo sorrow each time I climax. I cry silently during and after each of my sexual encounters. Funny, there are other times where thrill of doing it anywhere, anytime, and anyplace that gets me as high as any drug you could prescribe. If I had no one to conquer…I could conquer myself a hundred times a day."

"Where have you done it?" he asks in a perverted type of manner.

"Work, in the car, in my home, in the park, in the nightclub, in the grocery store bathroom, the changing room in the mall, and soon to be; your office. Anywhere the feeling comes –sorry no pun intended- over me is where the magic happens!"

"Do you like moments like that? He was too excited for me. Like doesn't he understand he's been exposed? He was rock hard by now.

"We are both sick. We are both in need of help. I know why I do, what I do. I want to have sex non-stop because I am trying to get something that was taken from me. I deserved to have that moment when I wanted it to happen, with whom…I wanted it to happen with. That shit fucked my head up. It made me want to kill myself; I hated myself to where I believed I deserved what happened. I had to stop at some point, because I realized no child deserved to have her body violated by someone who's mental stability; is distant like the moon. That's why I do what I do! Your reason would be…" I wanted to know all about him and there was no escaping me.

    "My wife is sick. Debra has cancer. I love her dearly. However, it has placed tremendous weight on me. I care for her with the utmost compassion, go to all the doctor appointments, and take care of our child. At the end of the day---I am still a man with needs. One evening, I started hunting for sex online. Next, a feeling of hellacious fire ignited on the inside of me. From that moment, I knew I was hooked. I too, think, sleep, and eat-*no pun intended*- sex." He had me wrapped in his story.

    "First, I thought it was a new form of sexual expression, or some form of youthful rejuvenation of my manhood. But it was more than that. It was if my mind had shifted. My mental state was not the same. I knew that I displayed all the classic symptoms of being addicted to sex. Lying to Debra about my whereabouts, being late picking up our daughter, taking time to sexually please myself while at work was shameful. Things were crazy because I was spending too much money for sex, or online entertainment. I knew it was bad when I was about to sleep with a hooker. Thoughts of sex were constant, like the blinking of a liar's eyes. Keeping you in therapy, for five years was a safe way to release. Your stories of excited passion, trimmed with the newness of having with strangers turned my thoughts into a sexual wonderland."

"You need help! You are out there more than me!"

"So do you!" he yelled back. At this point, he stared me down as if he wanted to do something.

"Like I told you, I am not coming back. I think there is something that can be prescribed to me without taking the soul of this woman away. I hate to hear what you are going through with your wife, but this--- this is wrong. I hopped on your lap to make you feel what I felt on my ninth birthday. It hurt, it violated, and it stripped away all of the innocence. At times I feel like such a whore." I shamefully confessed as I tried to pull myself off him.

"No!" He yelled as he leaned forward pulling me back on top of him.

"Since when have you been able to walk away from a moment of stimulating sex? You have needs and I have needs. We can fulfill them together." He quietly begs as he grabs hold of my breasts.

"David, you really don't want to do this. This is not right, this is not healthy." I begin to lose thought as he swallows my breasts into his warm mouth.

"I can't go there with you." I tried to talk myself out of wrong, but there I continued to straddle him as I arched my back.

It was as if my threat to stop seeing him unleashed a beast. I could not help it. My love below had been throbbing since I stepped out of my Rover. Now, it's swollen with a toxin, which if released…could be bad for us both. My insides were going mad. I was ready to re-lease and he was just as eager. He moved down my chest and circled around the pit of my belly as he took a deep dive downwards. My legs were spread as wide as tree roots. The throb-bing was so tremendous. I felt everyone in the building could hear it beating, as I lay upon the cheery wooden floor.

"Let me in. I need this as well. I can go for days. I can't seem to stop once it starts, the urges never dissolve."

"It's wide open and you're asking for permission?" I hope that this hoping he would hurry up and feed my need.

"Damn-" David slid in and took my body hostage. He held his own, and I climaxed about two times before he came. We switched positions and before I could find good position, I came again. His thrusts were long and powerful. The scattering of feet outside of the office mixed with the clad of calls that went unanswered in his office; excited us even more. *Now a sane, unbroken individual would jump up and refrain from their actions, fearing severe repercussions. Not us… we kept riding!*

"Hold all my calls Elaine. Mrs. Davis is breaking down. Call her prescriptions in to the first floor pharmacy. She will pick them up shortly." Without shortness of breath, he gave orders as he continued to pleasure. His focus on getting me to come again turned me on even more.

"I don't need passion, just a good fu----,"

"Don't say anything Jess, let's just do this until it runs out."

"Come now! We don't have time for that!" We continued until we both felt soreness.

As I cleaned up and gathered my things, he followed me to the door. The office reeked of sex. As I leaned to grab the door handle, he

*Londa B.*

grabbed my hand. All of a sudden, reality jumped back into my face.

"I can't see you anymore! What about our families, our children, our health, or our careers?" Now I sounded like the good doctor. Most of the people I sleep with, I never see them again. It's what I preferred. Again, I'm not looking for romance.

"People like us don't care about those things. We only think of ourselves. You and I both know our needs come before our wants. My hunger is insatiable! I don't have a cure for you or myself. With that being said, I will see you on this Thursday, around noon. Let Shirley know as you leave." He was cold and sterile. He went about fixing his office as nothing happened between the two of us.

"Yes, see you Thursday at noon. I guess this is our new norm, huh?"

"Something like that." He avoided eye contact with me.

"I guess we can screw ourselves to sanity until a new medication saves us." A sad joke, but I guess it was fine to go at it with someone just as crazy as me.

*What can I say? Hypersexually speaking...I need stimulation.*

28

Facts about Hypersexual (Hyperactive) Disorder

Hypersexual Disorder is where an individual has a constant desire for stimulation of the genital area. The problem occurs when the individual is unable to achieve long-term satisfaction. Shortly thereafter, the need for stimulation resurfaces.

There is a difference between someone with a high sex drive versus an individual with a hyperactive sex drive. The individual that has a high sex drive seeks seek with generally one person, several times a week. This person is also generally the aggressor within the relationship. For this person, pleasure is met and is sustained for a longer period length of time.

Someone with a hypersexual disorder will one, have more than one sexual partner. This act increases the chance to contract a STD. This individual will also seek sexual content/stimulation at any cost. The thought of sex is constant like the perpetual ticking of a Rolex. Sun up to the suns break into dusk, sex never exits the mind of the hyperactive individual. No long-term satisfaction appears to be in sight for this individual.

*Londa B.*

Signs of an individual with a hyperactive sex drive

- Constant need for stimulation. Constant masturbation, constant openness of sexual genital.
- Unable to stay in a monogamous relationship.
- Lies at any cost to obtain sex.

- Forgets or skips family functions to have sex
- Having sex with strangers, anytime, anyplace.

- Most bi-polar patients suffer from hypersexual disorders. Their desires for sex switch with their moods. In mania, they desire sex quite often, and in depressive states, there may be a reduced to zero want for sex.
- The desire with sex starts to interfere with family and work life.
- Excessive spending of money. Online porn, porn magazines, sexual favors, prostitutes, or escorts.

Treatment for Sexual (Hypersexual) Disorders

Having a hyperactive sex drive is a psychological disorder! This is not a condition, which someone chooses to do. This condition must receive treatment with the utmost care and professional help.

- The individual must receive a clinical evaluation by a trained and board certified psychiatrist.
- Psychotherapy may be required along with a medication regimen.
- Support, not criticism should be given. It's enough that the individual will be ashamed of their medical condition.
- They may also have fear instilled in self as well. Try to understand the condition from all points.

The agencies listed at the end of this book, will provide assistance in finding information and help one may need.

Londa B.

## Those Damn Voices!
## Schizophrenia at its worst...

*"Sanity remains defined simply by the ability to cope with insane conditions."*
-Ana Castillo

### Feb 27, 2006 Journal Entry #: 547

I don't know how to feel. My wife has left with the kids, and they do not trust me anymore. It seems I have lost all contact with the friends and family I thought were really in my corner. I lost *another* job a month ago, and the bills--- well I guess my wife decided to pay *her* bills and not mine! Lester (my dog) told me I should have killed her a long time ago! Lester said he saw it all happen, while I was at work.

**FUCK, FUCK, FUCKED!!!!** Now what do I do? What else can I say Mr. Journal? The doctor showed no sympathy as he told me my disease was progressive. Hell, I worked every day, came home to my family, helped around the house, watched TV, and slept. Doc's balls really must have swelled because he requested my ex-wife sit in on today's session. I call bull-shit! I saw the set-up...I saw it coming. He wanted to show her how *off* I was, so he could have her for himself!!! That bitch was there just to see me melt into puddle of nothing. Why couldn't she be strong and wait for me to get back on my feet?

I should have kept my damn mouth closed. No one had to know about the *flies* (the ones from Salvador Dali's artwork) that buzzed death, bad things, and the sins of others in my ears. The flies never lie. The flies represent decay and death amongst the earth! The flies buzzed secrets about how all my family members were talking about in my youth. How about the soldiers marching in front of me while taking me through my battles of the day! I swear I saw them and they steered me clear of enemies all day long!

Who would believe that? NO ONE! I was simply told I had a very creative mind. I was the last of five kids that had no one to interact with. My second to youngest brother is six years older than me. Were my parents not thinking of me? Oh…that's right, I was the accident no one wanted to happen."

I remember how in my senior year of high school, I sat naked in my room, talking to our local news anchor, Katie Miles about my new book release; *"Why Not?"* as I drank fine wine from a gold rimmed, crystal flute. Katie and I had something special. I looked good on TV too. I stayed up until three in the morning just to watch my interview. None of my friends believed my story; they just laughed and told me I would make a great comedian. Well, they were jealous!

I knew they were jealous because none of them came around or bothered to call me. My mothered figured it was a good thing to get me away from people. Not long after, I was able to graduate high school early. She failed to tell me what she had waiting on me.

She said the medicine would help me not to hear voices and do bad things- like kill my-self. Next, the downpour of cocktails was intro-duced. Since they started me on the medication, I haven't been right. The medicine never did anything except mummify me. Why not give me some weed? I loved the street drugs better! They gave me a better high and they didn't mess interfere with my sex drive!

Guessing since my wife and children left, I assume pulling a knife on them and chasing them around the house was the wrong thing to do. All I wanted to do was to show them how ugly their insides were!!!!! They treated me like dog shit. Why? I paid the bills, well no, I brought the money home, but hell, I was there. I think those voices are telling the truth!

*"They hate you Daniel! They do not appreciate you!"*

"Shut up----they do appreciate all that I do. She DID love me!"

*"Not how you think! She was sleeping with another man!"*

"Stop it! You don't know what you are talking about! My wife would never do that to me! Where are you, come tell me to my face."

*"You should kill yourself. Be with us, we will never talk about you. You're one of us."*

I wonder if that voice was right. With all that's going on, tonight will be a great night to kill myself! The Angel from most high has called for me! I have a greater mission in heaven more than here on earth! I have nothing left here on earth to accomplish. Everyone here does not see the big picture and they will drown in their own blood, once the earth has met its end. They are crazy- not me.

"Lord, do you really want me? If not, make these voices go away. I can't do this. I love my kids, I love my wife. Why is this happening? I can't take any more institutions, I

**Londa B.**

hate white walls and the dirty rooms. I hate
people who wear scrubs. They truly work for
the devil. No one is ever nice, or treats me with
dignity. I'm human. I hear how the medical
staff calls me crazy, or how they barely want to
touch me. Where is the real compassion?

The pills suck! All they do is leave my
mouth dry and tasting like I ate a plate of bat-
teries. I think a bullet would taste much better!
Please help me God!" I swear, if those doctors
perform one more shock treatment on me---I'll
kill them all! Let them see how it feels to be
shocked until you shit your pants and pass out!
After a while, those shock treatments don't do a
damn thing.

This is the end for me. I can't do this. No
wife, no job, no kids, no friends, and God never
wrote back! My mother is the only person in
the world that truly loves me.

My father shakes his head in disbelief,
but I know the voices and everything else is real. Why doesn't he believe me?"

I'm done...

*"Dear Mom,*

*I know you are upset with me, but the angels have called for me. I've already been informed of my assignment. The highest wants me to help all the families of the 9-11 incident heal and he also wants me to help all the other special people like me, come to his kingdom! I have a lot of work to do, so please don't cry out to Jesus asking him to bring me back to you. Once I am delivered to him---there is no coming back.*

*Tell Dad about my new job duties and tell the rest of that so-called family, that I WAS the winner after all. I know you did not cause any of this mom. It's not you! I know you loved me! You did well caring for me. As you know, the world is mad. Pray that your son does well on his first day in heaven. The Angels told me there was a lot to learn on the 1st day in Heaven Camp! I love you very much mom. You will be my shining star on earth---and I will be yours in heaven."*

*Your loving son,*

*Daniel*

*Londa B.*

Dear Diary,
May 12, 2006

My therapist said writing down my feelings would help me heal. My Lord! How can I
get through this? Daniel has finally succeeded
at killing himself. Little did I know, but the
procession to his funeral has already begun after his first attempt at suicide. I should have
known after his second attempt that he would
not stop until he killed himself. Now I'm here
grieving my last-born. He was too delusional to
be at home. No matter what medications we
gave him, it seemed to go straight through him.

I hate we took Daniel out of school so
early, but we were risking true embarrassment
within our own neighborhood and church. The
school allowed him to graduate early in Febru-
ary, so he wouldn't cause any more issues at
school. People knew something was wrong
with Daniel. And you know kids will be kids;
the bullying was beyond extreme. After leaving
school, life went on and Daniel seemed to get
better with a new regimen of medication. The
bad part about the medicine and all the effort
you put into trying to help, he still experienced
a lot of bad days. There were at least four other
times where my Daniel tried to kill himself.  I

feel guilty but I know deep down, I did all I could for my child.

Once we felt it was good for Daniel to return to gathering his education, we allowed him to go to college. Initially, we allowed Daniel to take online courses with only having to go to the college for mid-terms and finals. We only experienced a few problems, but it wasn't anything that was too hard for him. He was so smart! After that semester of success, we took Daniel to have his driver's license re-instated. He crashed his last car a year after he graduated from high school. Not only did he take too much of his medicine, but he was high on street drugs too. That boy was truly a handful but out of all my kids, he was my joy. Sounds funny but it's true. Even in his dark, confusing hours Daniel was everything to me.

That's enough for today.

"Carl, I should have never allowed Daniel to start going on campus for classes. I think back to when he met Heather. I question if he needed that *type* of situation, but what could I do? He would have eventually found some woman to be with.

"No, matter the condition, everyone wants to be in love as well as…"

"Carl, don't you say anything about sex."

"Well how do you thing we got grandkids here."

"I remember the first day we met her. I knew it was something about her, but I couldn't touch it even if my finger was on it!" Betty said as she knitted in her rocker.

"Betty Let it go. He's finally at peace. I miss my son too, but sweetie; it was too much stress and pain. We watched him suffer too much. I couldn't imagine living the life he did. Hell I get upset when I hear a fly buzzing rounds my ears. What would you do if you experienced what he did?"

"Carl, don't tell me how to get over my child!" Betty stopped rocking to put Carl in his place.

"I remember it like yesterday…"

*Daniel brings Heather home…*

"Hello Mrs. Adams. I'm Heather. Your son is truly amazing and oh- so smart." The stupid looking blonde said while she ran her hands through my son's hair. I could not believe how calm Daniel was around her. It was a calmness I'd never seen. It was a peaceful, not drug induced. I continued to monitor her behavior as she glided across my kitchen.

"How did you and my son meet?" I asked while trying to not show Daniel my eagerness to see his new lady friend out our home.

"We met in a marketing class." The ditz cheerfully answered.

"What is your major?" I asked. I hoped she would falter in her answer. I know those first year college students are somewhat undecided. College kids waiver in their studies, like flags in the wind.

"It's journalism ma'am." Heather responded with a smirk smeared across her face.

"Well that's great!" Maybe you can do a story on my son."

"What would that story be about ma'am?"

Londa B.

"You don't know Daniel do you? Have you noticed anything greatly odd about my son?" I asked reclining back in my kitchen rocker, while placing my good eye on her.

"Mom, stop! You don't need to do this!" Daniel pleaded as he began rocking in his chair.

"Well I am! I told you to be honest and tell people about your condition." I hated to do this, but there has yet to be a woman but me--- deal with Daniel.

"Daniel, what is it? What do you have to tell me that you haven't already told me? I promise to think with an open mind." She responded in a fake, *"I'll understand but I won't like it"* tone of voice while holding Daniel's hand.

"I have a mental disorder. I suffer with schizophrenia. It's a mental condition that has seemed to keep me more down than up in my life. I'm fine now and it's controlled. I visit my doctors and take my medicine, and that's all."

"Oh is that it? I have a cousin and a grandfather who suffered with the same disease. I can totally relate. It's nothing to be ashamed of. I hate the stigmas society places on people who suffer from mental illnesses. People fear what they don't know. Today's medicine and research are making things better." She naively responded.

"Is there a *FUCKING* cure?" I yelled in the strongest tone of voice I could mustard from the pits of gut! I knew this girl was trouble because I hadn't cussed like that in quite some time.

"Mother, please stop!" Daniel yelled, while shielding Heather as if she was under attack.

"There is only treatment, there is no damn cure. If you are going to be with my son, then you had better get educated real fast! This is a full-time relationship. If you can't hang and put the time in…then you are wasting your time!"

"Well then give me all the books you have! I'm not leaving Daniel, we have something special. He told me this would be a challenge, but he didn't know I was a team player! Now I understand what he means by challenge."

"Are you talking about me?" Betty sat on the edge of her rocker.

"No I'm not; I just know what I have ahead of me."

"It's going to be okay love. I dreamt of you before you even appeared to me. We will be okay." She cooed as she rubbed my son's reddened face.

*Londa B.*

With those last words, she grabbed my sons hand and they both left without one word. I guess you can say that was the night my son, became a man.

Dear Diary
May 21, 2006

"I had to take a little time to cry my face off. I miss my son! I got through packing his room today. The Goodwill will be here soon. I was finally able to rid the last batch of bill collectors. I could not believe the attitude of those collectors. What in the hell was I suppose to do? Go to his grave and drag him out, so he can pay his bills? They had no sympathy; all they wanted was proof of his death. Well he's free and clear of all the bullshit. Heather is upset the bill collectors are coming after her. Oh well, she had it coming, she made all the debt.

Since Daniel hung himself, we could not collect on his insurance policy, so we paid out of pocket for his service.

## Day of Daniels Service

    I have not seen my grandkids since two months before Daniel took his life. I could not believe this hussy brought some jerk to Daniel's funeral. I collected myself, because my grandkids were there to say their good-byes to their father. I smelled their hair, caressed their faces, and held their hands tightly. I held onto them as long as I could because I didn't know when would be the next time I saw them.

    That day was bittersweet. I hated seeing her, but I got to see my grandchildren. Out of all these years, I tried to raise my children well. We were a nice family, with good catholic values, decent jobs and a nice home. What made my boy drag this *thing* home?

    "Maw-Maw, mommy is going to leave us with you." Timothy quietly announced while staring at his father as he lay in his casket.

    "No, she would never do that Timothy. Sarah, you keep your brother in line! It will be okay, your mother and I will work out some arrangements."

    I prayed before approaching her. I couldn't do that without the help of The Lord. I turned to see Heather standing behind me.

"Did Timothy tell you the deal?" she asked in a stale voice. *Whew, she reeked of vodka.*

"I smelled the truth in the air." I acknowledged her drunkenness, knowing what was about to flow from her cracked, dry lips.

"Why are you leaving your children? Why are you doing this?" I questioned, but she kept lowering her face from reason."

"Sarah is *off* and I think Lil Timmy is on the way to becoming a knock off the old block"

**~SLAP!**

Licking the blood from her lips Heather carried on.

"Their items will be delivered to your house tomorrow. The movers are paid for two hours. That's all I could afford. I can't watch my children turn into their father. I thought I could handle it years ago Betty, but I failed. I never knew the amount of work, patience, and love it would take. Truthfully, I never cared or took care of my family members that suffered from Schizophrenia. I guess the stigmas in the back of my mind prevented me from really wanting to care for them. I hope you believed that there was a time where I loved your son."

"I tried to tell you that, but cupids bow was clean up your ass. Mothers know their

children? You hurt more than you helped."
Heather was quiet.

"You drove him to his grave. You were
always dogging and pushing him to the edge.
He may have been unsettled, but he knew you
were cheating on him. If you cared, you would
have never given up on him, or your marriage."

"Betty, Daniel was losing jobs as soon as
he started them. He did not perform well at
work. His clients were tired of him not respond-
ing, and they took their business elsewhere! He
could barely get out of the bed most days!
Don't forget the stunt with the knife. Betty, I
was taking care of him *and* the kids."

"That's what a wife does."

"I thought he was turning into a lazy
slob, but that wasn't the case. Like you, I did all
I could."

"You should have called when he started
to spiral out of control! All the signs were
parked between your eyeballs. You kept him
from us until he was too much to handle! In addition, the coroner found traces of drugs and
alcohol in his system. Whose idea was that?"

"Daniel became so distant from us within
the last couple of years. It seemed he only came
alive when he was drinking or doing drugs! He
*wanted* me in the bedroom and I missed that.
He was always zonked out somewhere, when
on those meds. I was lonely."

"You are such a stupid one!" I screamed as I swung her around the corner wall.

"Drugs and alcohol make people with schizophrenia VIOLENT! Daniel had a past with drugs growing up." I screamed out while shaking Heather like a rag doll. *She's about to be lying right next to Daniel in a few minutes!*

Crying and on her knees Heather started to shake beyond control. "I watched the man I fell in love with, turn into a cold and dead-eyed stranger. There were times where I stood before your son, naked and he did not respond. I felt less than a woman." All Heather could do was cry. My feelings were all over the place. One minute I want to kill her and the next I want to forgive and promise all would be well.

"It's okay. Please sweetheart, let's talk about this later. You have a lot on your mind. Go take a vacation, and call the kids daily to let them know how much you love them. Please do not give up on your children, like the people who gave up on our Daniel. Let Daniel's life be an example. We all have learned something through Daniel's death."

"Okay, I will give it a try." Heather did not stay for Daniels service, and the kids didn't seem to be bothered by her absence.

We never saw Heather again. Carl and I are raising our grandchildren. It's a challenge, but I would rather them be with us than anyone else. I use my faith so much where re-fills are necessary. Church has become my second home. Those last few years I spent with my son, after he moved back home; were special.

Daniel stayed away from anyone who lived outside our home. Carl and I were tired of fighting to get home to go to the doctor. We couldn't handle him. Daniel didn't like to talk much either. He did good enough to continue writing in his journal or paint. Now that I sit and read his final journal entries, they were disturbing. At some points, they made no sense.

When Daniel allowed us to, Carl and I tended to him with bathing and trying to get him to eat. The hallucinations drove Daniel insane. I caught him one night trying to open his brain with my kitchen knife. It was my fault; I forgot to put the lock back on the drawer!

Screaming the whole time while in route to the hospital, Daniel cried about the insides of his brain being full of worms and maggots. It took Carl and our next-door neighbor, Jerry, along with his teenage son, to pin Daniel down the whole ride. This was one of our many nights of hell.

The only time we rested through the night, was when Daniel was committed. I guess we all can rest now.

*"Daniel, it's your star here on earth. Momma loves you. Sarah and Timothy miss you. It' not a day that that passes where we fail to talk about you. Do well in your new assignment. Keep an eye out for your children as well. They truly loved you, son. I'll be okay, don't worry about me. I'm doing just fine. You and your angelic buddies, keep that midnight sky sparkling. I know you have peace now. It's all over, no more voices."*

"I opened my heart to tell you about our son. Daniel was once active, happy, and willing to live life at its fullest. Unfortunately, his disease became worse when he stopped going to the doctor, stopped his meds and back on drugs and alcohol. We tried, but it was so hard.

People don't understand mental illnesses. Daniels paranoia was extreme. I distanced myself from family members who talked about how his death was preventable. No one knew anything. No one walked the walk we did. When you get to the point of wanting to end it all, nothing is on that person's mind, except making the pain go away! I wish those bastards could experience ten minutes of my son's life. They would have died within the first five. Daniel was indeed a trooper!"

Londa B.

## <u>Fact about Schizophrenia</u>

- Schizophrenia is a chronic, severe, and disabling brain disorder. This disorder affects 1 percent of Americans.
- People with schizophrenia suffer from many types of delusions. Certain tastes, smells, sounds, feelings, and sight, Can send a person into a stage of paranoia. You may re-call how Daniel heard and saw things. Or how he felt things inside of his body. Most delusions are very far-fetched and impossible. However, to the inflicted, it is all VERY REAL.
- Alcohol and drugs should not be in use by an individual with schizophrenia disorder. This worsens their moods and makes them aggressive and/or violent.
- Schizophrenia usually emerge in men, in their late teens and early twenties. For women, in their mid twenties to early thirties.
- Some children as young as five years of age have been diagnosed as having schizophrenia. The signs

could range from change in sleep patterns, and change in friends. In diagnosing youth, one must be very careful because many symptoms listed previously mock puberty and social issues youth experience.

- Most people who suffer with paranoid schizophrenia try to commit suicide. The voices, the medications, and the confusion, along with the lack of support/love from family drives the individual away. Next, contemplation of suicide occurs.

- Chemical imbalances of neurotransmitters (dopamine and glutamate) plays a role in schizophrenia.

- Symptoms of schizophrenia fall into three broad categories.

Positive Symptoms- These symptoms entail weird thoughts or perceptions. Including; hallucinations, delusions, thought disorder, and disorders of movement.

*Londa B.*

<u>Negative Symptoms-</u> These display a loss or decrease in the ability to carry out job assignments or daily life duties. Initiate plans, speak, express emotions, or finding pleasure in everyday life. Now some people may deem this as a sign of laziness or depression, but only a trained professional will be able to identify a patient with schizophrenia.

<u>Cognitive symptoms</u> (known as cognitive deficits) are problems where the individual has problems with attention, memory, planning and organizing skills are close to depletion. These effects can be the most hardest to identify, but yet they are the most disabling to the individual, due to the loss of living a normal life.

For more information about schizophrenia disorders, refer to the websites in the back of the book.

### Bi-polar... Now What?
### Author Londa B.

*"The pleasure of criticizing robs us of the pleasure of being moved by some very fine things."*
La Bruyere, *Les Caracteres*


Who in heaven took the wings off the Angels and allowed the devils roam the earth? Where did my Angel, my protection go? Walking out of my doctor's office with no *real* outlook on how to live my life, as a newly diagnosed patient with bi-polar disorder, shook me...as well as my faith, to the core. I thought I was okay. I thought it was stress with a side plate of depression.

There were times where I felt as if the word, *"bi-polar"* was just as bad as saying terminal cancer or HIV. Could I be exaggerating a little bit? I don't think so, because society would be more understanding and knowledgeable about other illnesses. Mental illness- that's a different story. Answer this, do you see many people being open or comfortable to discuss mental illness? Sad to say, people announce worse things on Facebook, but when it comes to posting about a tragedy related to mental illness, folks announce their prayers, then move onto commenting about some insignificant post. Where did we go wrong? We talk more than we do. Change has to happen.

Years ago, divine intervention halted this wife and devoted mother of three from committing suicide. Being raised as a preacher's kid, I was taught to believe, only The Lord could give, and take life. If you committed suicide- you go to hell. I never want to walk down *Suicide Lane*.

After the birth of my second daughter, post-partum depression was kicking my ass. One night in route to my job, I had a hell-awful breakdown. It was so severe to where I was sure I wouldn't live to tell about it. I wanted to drown all the pain my mind and body harbored. As I approached the McKinley Bridge, tears stared to flow and I couldn't believe how bad I was shaking. My breathing was rapid and I went into a panic attack. Always being fearful of bridges, I lost it, and decided to pull over. I veered over to the right, and saw the Mississippi River covered with its first layer of winter snow.

As I got out my car, the winter air fiercely wisped across my face and through my hair. Normally a night so cold would charge me to fight the cold, but I didn't. My body was numb. Footsteps from my car door to the railing of the bridge proved I gave zero damns about my fear of bridges. The rivers current mesmerized me, and taking the plunge was the only way to stop the pain.

Before I came to this point, I viewed suicide as a selfish act. I thought about all my loved ones who would be left behind. I thought of pain and grief I would cause to those who loved me. But as I looked back on my life, I wanted to stop being a burden to my loved ones. I wanted my family to live without me. I figured they would be better off. Now as I crossed the railing, my hands held tight to the cold steel. I was sad and wanted to end my pain. As I closed my eyes to pray- I heard a man call out to me. It was a cop.

He was calm and really nice. He asked me what was wrong and what could he do to help me. I just stared at him crying. He began talking to me about second chances. He told me that I would never know what my life would really be like if I chose to end it. He asked if I had kids or family. I nodded, yes. He said he was sure they would love to see their mother in the morning. He carried on to how I would miss many birthdays, weddings, and possibly grandchildren.

I couldn't stop crying. As he slowly approached, he asked if I knew The Lord and could he pray with me. When he said that- I thought back to all of my father's sermons and the promise of hell awaiting me once I killed myself.

With that, I crossed back onto solid ground. As I turned around to thank the officer, he was gone. Puzzled, I looked as far up and down that bridge to find his car. Walking back to my car- I noticed only one set of tire tracks. Scared, I jumped in my car. I looked and hoped the officer would return with an ambulance or escort me home. Then it hit me- it wasn't an officer, it was an Angel. With that, I called off work, and I drove myself straight to the Mercy Hospital. After sharing my story, I was admitted to the psychiatric ward.

I was placed on a forty-eight hour hold. As I was released, I was given a prescription for antidepressants. They helped, but I still felt as if something was wrong. It wasn't until seven years later and a new doctor, that I would find out what continued to pain me for so many years.

Fast forward to present day, I feel great. Yes, there are days when I feel a little heavy, but I always believe, if The Lord brings you to it…you will get through it. My marriage and career is much better. I couldn't do any of this without the desire to get better, a great circle of support and one her of a medical team! While there is no cure, this disease is manageable, but you have to do your part. My passion to actively advocate for those with mental health issues as well as mental health reform, is undeniable.

Facts about Bi-Polar Disease:

➢ Over 10 MILLION people in America suffer from bi-polar disorder. There is no certain sex it heavies on. The disease affects men and women the same.

Bi-polar disease causes mood swings from overly energetic to being very low and sad. When an individual is in a *manic episode* it may cause and individual to:

- Feel really happy or very irritable
- Possess a very high opinion of self
- No need for a lot of sleep
- Talk more than usual.
- Have racing thoughts.
- Become overactive performing daily activities. Does more than the usual.
- Feel that it's difficult to concentrate on jobs at hand.
- Be easily distracted by sights and sounds.
- Impulsive actions occur. The individual starts to live a life of recklessness. Things like, going on shopping sprees, driving recklessly, partaking in foolish busi-

ness ventures, or having frequent, indiscriminate sex.
- There is a less need for sleep. The individual does NOT experience fatigue.

What one may experience when dealing with depression.

- Feelings of sadness or anxiousness for a significant amount of time.
- Feeling of hopelessness or displaying a pessimistic attitude.
- Slow thoughts and speech due to extreme tiredness.
- Suicidal thoughts.
- Decreased interest in usual activities as well as having sex.
- Poor display of eating and sleeping habits.
- Restlessness or extreme irritability.
- Change in sleeping (more or less) patterns.

People must understand that there are different types of Bi-polar disorder. Your physician will determine which type you are, based on your **HONEST** answers you provide during your consultation. Honesty is the best policy for the correct diagnosis.

*Londa B.*

**Bipolar I:** Type I is considered the classic form. This type of disorder causes recurrent reruns mania and depressive states. Depressed stated could last for a short period or last for months. After depressive stated the individual could go back to feeling fine, or they could go right into another manic mode. There are frequent amounts of manic episodes in the type.

**Bipolar II:** In this type of disorder, the individual will still suffer from the depressive states, but the episodes of mania are less severe.

**Mixed States:** This is where the individual experiences mania and states of depression at the same time. Now during this stage, the depressed mood is an activator for a manic episode.

**Rapid Cycling:** In this case, the individual has four or more episodes within a 12-month period. Therefore, the individual gains the label of having bi-polar disorder with rapid cycling.

If you think, you or someone in your family may possess some of these traits or characteristics monitor them, by keeping a mood diary. At the end of your evaluation period, talk with your loved one. Please be sure to do this with ease, compassion and gentleness. See if they want help or an evaluation by a medical professional. Do not let moments like this fly by. Could you live with the guilt for the rest of your life, if your loved one did the *unthinkable* act? Stop with the stigmas and biased thoughts about mental health issues and the people who live with them.

*"Mental illness is nothing to be ashamed of, but stigma and bias shame us all!"*

Former U.S. President- Bill Clinton

### Her Depression Filled Life

*"There are many who dare not kill themselves for fear of what their neighbors will say."*
-Cyril Connolly, *The Unquiet Grave*

"Rachel baby, wake up! Come on baby, not again! I thought things were going better! Don't do this to us, come on baby----please WAKE UP! Danielle! Go get the phone and call 911! Hurry up! Come back when you're done and help me with your mother!"

"Okay dad, they're on the way! The operator is on the phone. The speaker is on."

"Mr. McMichael is your wife breathing? Have you checked for a pulse?"

"You know this is not the first time we have been on *this* block. She has a pulse, but it's weak! How long before the ambulance arrives?"

"Soon Mr. McMichael, check her pulse again!"

"She's not breathing!"

"Start CPR Mr. McMichael!"

Compressing my solid frame onto my wife's frail chest, while trying to blow life back into her lungs, was an act I have done one too many times! I'm trying to think of what could have pushed her the edge again.

"Excuse me sir, we need space! We'll take this over now, thank you." The strong, and confident paramedic said.

"Buck, go ahead and place the pads on her, I'm going to start and IV and get fluids wide open!"

"Got it, pads are on, I'll set the voltage, how much we going?"

"She's losing color and she's not breathing, do 400 then go up from there!"

"CLEAR!" the paramedic yelled.

The electrifying shock shook my wife's body. I saw her face twitch, then her head turned. The monitor showed rhythm, but without normality. Soon, she stopped breathing again.

"Take her to 600! She's flat lining again! The other medic announced.

"CLEAR!" the paramedic checked Rachael's pulse. Looks like she's back.

"Okay, IV is flowing, blood is drawn and heart rate is low at about 40 beats per min. and her BP is damn low...60/40! Let's get her tubed." Mr. McMichael, did you find what she took?" Buck asked as he worked non-stop.

"Her usual cocktail! Oxycodone, Xanax, Seroquel, and sleeping pills!"

"Get the medicine bottles Mr. McMichael, we are heading out! Dispatch, this is driver 342, in route to Tallahassee Medical. Approximate ETA time--- twelve minutes. Patient is an African American female, thirty-nine years of age, five feet four inches-"

"How much does your wife weight?"

"About one hundred and thirty."

"Husband stated that the patient took an excessive amount of Xanax, Seroquel, sleeping pills, and Oxycodone. Patient was shocked two times, to revive the heart. Epinephrine has been given, and patient is intubated. Fluid is wide open, heart rate, as well as blood pressure, are still unstable at this moment. Last BP was 40/60 and her heart rate is currently only 47 beats per minute. We are now in route, ten minutes until arrival. State if there are any diversions on the way." Terry commanded.

"You are clear 342, see you in ten. Trauma team is prepared and on standby for your arrival. Over and out!" Damn Terry and Buck were good at their jobs. How does Rachael manage to do this on the nights they work?

"What the hell? Loosen these damn straps, Darren!" Rachel screamed as she wrestled about.

"NO! Earlier you kept trying to pull your tubing out. After you were good enough to breath on your own, you kept trying to hurt yourself. I plan on talking with the nurse who left her pen on your tray. That's why your neck is bandaged."

"Leave me alone!"

"Miss, could you leave the room?" The sitter left without word.

"You have pushed me to my limits woman! I've read the books, I've attended the sessions with you, and I have been there one hundred percent! Your child has cared after you more than you have cared after her. You need to work harder at this Rachael, or this marriage is over! I never wanted to say this to you, but this stunt you pulled leaves me speechless. I'm tired of Danielle being embarrassed, because her friends witness her mother, *once again*, being carried out on stretcher. Do you ever think of our child? I don't want our child to be scarred by this madness. She needs the both of us." Rachael continued to stare out the window as if I wasn't there.

Now standing in front of his wife, Darren gave his last speech. "Right now, the only thing you're teaching our daughter is that it's okay to take the easy way out. You're teaching her that it's better to die than to deal with life. What in the hell keeps you from being happy, baby? I thought we shared everything with one another. That is what you loved about me and vice versa."

"I don't care to talk."

"Rachael, you know I love you, but these acts of suicide are pushing me away. I don't know if it's me, our daughter, your parents or work, but you need to tell me something!" Not even for a cup of water, Rachael wasn't going to open her mouth. I called for the sitter to return. I grabbed my jacket, stopped at the front desk to inform them on when I would return and went home to our child. Rachael needed rest. I have tried the nice guy approach, now it's time to get tough!

"Dad, is mom---still alive?" Danielle quietly asked.

"Yes, she is, thank God!"

"Great, God failed to answer my prayers!" Danielle screamed as she masked her tears with her hands.

"What in the hell are you talking, girl! You're mother is sick and you know that! You wishing her dead will only decrease your days of life on this earth. What in the hell has gotten into you?" I asked frantically, while shaking life out of our fourteen-year-old daughter.

"Stop it! You would not understand! You save her ass every time! Time after time, she does the same shit and each time---you act like it's the first time! If she really wanted to kill herself, she' should do it when we're not home. That way when we find her, it will be too late! She does this to make us miserable like her."

"Do not think for one minute, fourteen means twenty-one! You better watch what you say!"

"Dad, I love mom, but she is making me sad, she is never there like she used to be, she is always sleeping, or in some type of pain. Whenever she is up, it's only for a minute and she's back off to bed. Does she love me?"

"You know you're mother loves you sweetie."

"My friends are always talking about our family. I'm tired of it dad!"

"They're stupid and they have no under-standing about of life. I'm here for you. How do you think I feel? I'm a Doctor, and I can't save my own wife. How do you think I feel when I go to my place of work, to sign your mother in? You think I'm happy about that? Outside of all the drama, we do pretty well.

We have a nice home, your mom and I make a great living and you have the best of everything.

"Dad, none of that matters if we're not happy. I want my mom back. I know we're not exempt from the challenges of life, but this is too much!"

I know it's hard for her to continue her success with her books, her radio show and her artwork. Maybe that's why she's upset. Something happened along the way. She's just not telling us. Danielle you're right. People can have the best of things and still be unhappy. Just know God has us covered. Baby girl, your mother's depression is serious. We are going to do all we can to help her. Now is not the time to ignore her."

"Okay, can I go stay with granny and papa this week? I want to enjoy my spring break."

"Get packed, I'll call them to come pick you up."

"Thanks Dad! I'm sorry what I said about mom. I guess even if it meant I would be sad, I just wanted her pain to end."

I grabbed my child and held her close to my heart. This child provides strength when I need it most. I love her.

"Dad understands, I'll be here as long as the good Lord allows. We all will help mom get back on track. She has so much to offer, and a

lot of people love and depend on her. Now go
pack, I need to clean up around here a little before I head back to your mother."

A few days passed and I had not called
Rachael. This wasn't the norm for me, but I
wanted to try a different approach with her. She
needed to know how upset I was. I tried to re-
fresh myself by reading my bible but the phone
rang.

"Dr. McMichael?"

"Yes, who's calling?"

"It's Dr. Lee. Your wife has requested
your presence. She's up and about and is doing
much better. We removed her from the medical
floor and she's currently been transferred to
the…"

"Yes, I know where she's at."

"We're having a session this afternoon.
She finally submitted herself to group and individual therapy. It's been a struggle but she's
taking her medications now. I see something
different about Rachel this time, and truthfully I
think a change is on the horizon."

"I'm on the way!"

"Great, see you then."

"Hey Rachael, how are you doing?" I
asked while looking her over.

"Baby, I'm fine. Seriously, I am tired of this shit. I the hate pain, I hate being sad for such extended periods of time. Who knew the hands of time could extend so far out."

We both laughed. I sensed an old sweetness from my wife. She hasn't made me laugh in a long time. Her hair was a cherry cola red, and her skin was a glossy coat of vanilla glazed with golden honey. Her cat like, eyes blinked out beautiful hues of hazel. Wow, she looked good. Her scent drove me crazy, but I knew I had to stay on course.

"You look great." I stated as I took my wife into my arms and held her as tight as I could. I was overjoyed that I could still see her, hear her laugh and hold her hand.

"Thank the sitter. She put me together with the stuff you left for me. You look good too." She hinted while looking directly at my crotch.

"Damn baby, you for real?" I asked in with the excitement of a schoolboy. With it being so long, I was ready to take her in the bathroom for a few minutes. I missed the intimacy between us. I could never engage in sex with her, while she was zonked out on her medicine. Today though, I was ready for a little one on one with my wife.

"Yes, I'm for real. I know you haven't been *fed* in months. Please tell me I can make that up to you." She begged as she leaned over and grabbed herself a handful.

Damn, I wanted to go in at that moment, but I reserved myself.

"Baby, let's focus on you getting better and doing things one day at a time. How do you feel? I want to know what we need to work on." I questioned while holding her close.

"I need the help. I need someone to stay on me to take my medication. I have to get through the adjustment phase and after that, I know everything will be okay!"

"What happens when you go back to writing or painting?

I know, I know. It's hard at times because I feel like the medications interrupt my creative flow. Not to mention, it kills my sex drive."

"You know I love you no matter what. It's not about the sex." My hardness said otherwise.

"I never fell out of love with you. Please know that. I always heard of shock treatments and became curious."

"Why shock therapy. You're nowhere near in need of that."

"Well I was wondering if they could shock my stuff back to life, if it dies after being put back on this medicine." Rachael died in laughter as she hid her face under the sheet."

"Woman you are too much!"

"You know what really got to me?'

"What?"

"People stopped showing up to my ex-hibits, my sales suffered and several of my gal-leries were closed. Even my last book failed to live to its expectations. Seeing the reviews my readers left; broke me to the core.

"You know what they say about the dead, right?

"Go ahead- say it Rachael."

"You're worth more dead than alive."

"Not funny! You will be back on top again."

"Yeah, on top of you." Rachael couldn't keep her hands off me.

"Stop woman." I stood and turned away. I didn't want her to see me long as a pole. That would give her a reason to keep going. I need to see if Dr. Lee would send her home with plenty of whatever he gave her. Rachael was happy.

What she said about being more valued after death was the truth. Sad but true. You never miss it until it's gone.

"Okay, let's get those creative juices flowing again. We can take yoga, we can travel or do whatever is necessary."

"Sounds good to me."

"You know, it's time we remodel the house. I'm going to call Damon to come over and look at doing something special with your office."

"How about a huge bay window facing the lake. I would love that. Four walls depress the hell out of me."

"One thing I know, Damon will get the job done. How about a surround sound system? I know how you love Raheem DeVaughn, Jilly from Philly, Kem, Floetry and the Chronicles."

"You would do that baby?"

"Hey, are you serious about staying on track?"

"Yes, but I'm scared to see Danielle."

"Why do you say that?"

"I saw our child, standing right over me shaking her head. I felt as if she was deciding if she was going to help me, or let me die! I felt like a loser. I felt like I failed at being a mother."

I could not tell my wife how Danielle felt. I didn't want to pull her back into that deep abyss of depression. She was in a good place.

"Baby, they had already shocked you a few times, plus injected reversal drugs to halt the overdose from taking you to the grave. You were seeing things."

"I never want Danielle to see that again. I want to be a good mother, and wife. Darren, I am so sorry I put you through so much."

"It's okay."

"No matter how much time passes, the past is always present in my life. The rape by my uncle, the abuse from my ex, and the loss of my twin sister, wrecks my soul. I try to move onward, but the pain comes in waves."

"It's okay. I've been here for you, and I understand what you went through. I may not be able to *feel* your pain, but I understand. What you need to do is take pride in the fact that you are a survivor. Get up, let me show you something.

I took my wife to the plastic mirror that seemed to stretch our looks beyond recognition, but the picture was very clear.

"You are still standing! You have confidence; you have courage, grace and undeniable beauty. Please make this the last time you try to take the gift of life away. You have a lot to live for."

She smiled until her face hurt. Rachel turned around and placed her temple against my mine.

"Through Christ we can do all things! I pray that I live to the end with you, and I pray that this medication along with the good Lord, delivers me."

"Amen! I'm loving the new you. Let's get this session going."

"Okay!"

I'm proud of my wife. She decided to live and her actions showed it. These past few years were rough for all of us. From my parents, to her parents and our daughter, this has been one hell of a trip. Through it all, prayers never ceased. If it wasn't for our faith in God, our parents and close friends- we might've all jumped overboard.

*"There's only one corner of the universe you can be certain of improving, and that's your own self.*
-Aldous Huxley, Time Must Have a Stop

Londa B.

## Cut One...Cut Two...Cut Three!
## I Love Cutting!
## Meagan Williams

*"For the first time in months, I felt together. Sharp. In hurting myself, I had at last found a way to release the pressure.*
*But it was more than that. I was now different. I felt different. I'd discovered a way to control my feelings. Just because self-mutilation wasn't deemed an acceptable coping mechanism didn't mean I was going to stop doing it."*
–Victoria Leatham, *Bloodletting: A Memoir of Secrets, Self-Harm, and Survival*

Ah, this is why I do what I do. The stresses of the day need releasing! I could not imagine having all this bullshit build up in me. I try to talk things out, I try to write shit out, and all I end up with is pictures of razor blades and drops of blood on the paper. I feel better as I take the small, but yet deadly 1x2 sharp piece of steel, and glide it across my arm, three to ten times. Sometimes I pass out from watching my blood trying to coagulate from the incisions on my forearm. Before passing out, feelings of elevating to another level is better than smoking weed. Cutting is the only way I can cope with the shit going on around me.

As I bleed out, I can feel all the drama and the bullshit spill from my body. Once that blood pools onto my forearm, I feel satisfied knowing misery and pain is leaving my body. I guess cutting is better than a bullet to the dome, or snapping my neck as I try to hang myself. That suicide shit doesn't always go as planned. Two of my friends failed at suicide and now their parents care for them. They're complete vegetables.

Ally tried to hang herself and failed. Her mother heard the chair fall over in the attic. When she made it to the attic, she saw Alley hanging and grasping for the hand of death. She kicked and bucked her eyes at her mother, hoping she would leave her alone. Later, the doctor delivered the news that Alley had too much "hang time". I could not believe that her mother brought her home! Where is the fucking quality of life?

And my friend Malcolm, well he shot himself and hit some part of his brain that controls motor skills and speech. Can you imagine his luck? Again, another friend with no quality of life. Who wants to wipe drool away, give daily baths, change diapers or deal with feeding tubes? I think their parents were a combination of nuts and selfish for keeping their kids around like that.

I was pissed when my mother found out about me cutting myself. For a while, she believed I was rough playing with our two hundred and twenty pound Mastiff, Sir Duke, and our Persian cat, Egypt. I always wore long sleeves, no matter what time of the year it was. I always locked the bathroom door and I never allowed my mom to see me naked. She's always wearing her goody two shoes. She judges before she asks.

She actually caught me in the act late one night. I forgot to lock my door. Hell, she must have eaten light that night, because her steps were as light as a ballerina on her tip-toes.

"Meagan? What are you doing! Give me your arm!" she commanded as if she was operating on a patient.

"Get out of my room and get your damn hands off me! You could not even begin to understand why I do what I do! I'm tired of keeping this shit a secret anyways!"I raged while throwing things at her.

"Stop it Meagan! Do you think I am going to allow you to do whatever the hell you'd like, under my roof?"

"Get out of my room right now!" I screamed hoping she would not call my dad into the matter.

"Peter, get up!"

"What is it? Why all the yelling?" My dad looked bothered.

"Get the keys and get the car ready! Meagan needs to go to the hospital." Next, thing I knew my Dad was doing exactly what she said without a single word. He never questions anything. He simply moves along as if he really doesn't care what happens in this house. He's just here to pay bills and do what she says. I wish there were more 'us' time, like it used to be, when I was younger! I guess those days are behind us.

"Get your ass up, put on some jeans and grab your jacket. I don't know what the hell you could be going through at seventeen, but if you keep doing this up, you will not see your next birthday!"

"I hate you!" I shouted as I hurried to grab my clothes."

"No, you hate yourself! You know there are no secrets in this house. We ask you guys about things in school and with your friends. Your dad and I do our best to keep an open door! No topic is off limits with us! I wish you guys come to us, rather than going to one of your young, dumb-assed friends. I understand that there will be moments where you guys don't tell us everything, but the stuff that mat-

ters, the stuff that can change your life in an in-
stant; you should need to talk to us!"

"You don't listen. You only talk. You
have no idea what it's like to be a teen these
days." Trying to prove a point to this woman is
a lost cause.

"Times are bad. This isn't when your father and I was growing up." Young girls are
coming up pregnant, teens are being diagnosed
with HIV, and sex trafficking and racial profil-
ing is out of control! This world is a mess. I
can't allow something to happen to you guys."

"You are not as with it as you think."

You listen to me! It's our job as well as
our right, to parent you until your asses move
out! Now get your ass to the car! We have to
ride past two hospitals, just so my co-workers
don't get wind of this! No one needs to know
our business."

The ride was long and quiet. Truthfully, I
was scared. I didn't know what was going to
happen. All I could think about was never being
able to glide that razor across my forearm or
wrist, to release my pain. Yeah, mom's is right.
Things have changed for sure. Keeping up with
the 'in' crowd, looking a certain way, weighing
a certain weight, drives me crazy. People are
mean and no one cares until something happens
to them. Why can't people be liked for who
they are?

"Hi, I'd like to speak with someone in your intake department. My daughter needs a mental health evaluation." I could tell my mother was embarrassed. It was a voice I had never heard her speak in.

"Start filling out these forms, and bring your insurance card back, when you are done." The overworked registration clerk requested as she peered over her silver frames at me. I pulled my sleeves down, to hide scars.

"I need assistance for a pick-up to room twenty."

Who hired this linebacker? A man standing about six feet four inches towered over me as if I was a bug close to being smashed. This job isn't for him. He needs to be bouncing at some nightclub, or signing up with the NFL. I noticed a short stubby security guard following us. Talk about role reversal.

"Okay, Meagan, let's do this the easy way. No one wants to break a sweat or stir up the scenery. All we want to do is keep you for a few days. We want to help you, but we need to evaluate you. So please, gather your stuff, allow Tyrell to seat you in the wheelchair and we will be on our way." The security guard made his request clear.

"I need to have a female nurse assist her in changing her clothes, and taking her personal items. Meagan, you will have to go with the nurse. She will give you a pair of scrubs, and footies to keep your feet warm. You will have to remove all jewelry. You cannot take your phone with you. This is for your safety.

I looked over to my mother and she nodded to me as if it was okay. For the first time in a while, my dad and I made eye contact. This was the first time we have seen each other in a while. I could tell that he was hurt as well as confused, but suddenly guilt rode in and he dropped his head. Does he realize that I still want to be his little girl? Does he realize how much I miss spending time together?

"Will they keep me long? I don't want to be here forever. This place will not become my new mailing address! I refuse that!" The nurse consoled me and told me helping myself is the first step in recovery. She talked as if I was there for some AA group.

Tyrell and the security guard were quiet in route to my room. We had to be buzzed through many doors. For a second, I felt as if I was on my way to jail.

"Hello Meagan. I'm Doctor Reynolds's. I'm sure you don't like your surroundings, but you will adapt."

"No I won't. This place is cold and sterile."

"Meagan, can you provide me with a summary of what's going on? Do you feel something is missing from your life? Please be honest. I can't help you if you don't tell the truth. You have nothing to fear. The doctor sat back and waited for me to respond.

"Look, things are tough. I feel too much peer pressure, I hate how my family has changed since the death of my brother. It's like he never existed. My parents never talk about him. All his pictures were out one day and the next; they were gone. My dad has drowned in a pool of work and my mother…"

"Go on."

She is a 'holic' of everything! Alcoholic, workaholic, talkaholic, bitchaholic---you name it, that's her."

Are those even words? The doctor joked.

"You're funny.'

"And you're smiling."

"My family has divided a long time ago. I live in a house full of strangers who so happen to know a little about each other."

"That's a lot. I understand you're into cutting. How do you feel when you cut?"

"I feel like hell slides out of my veins. It feels like a real good high. I guess I focus on the cut more than my problems. I could never seem to address my problems face to face, so besides my razors, writing does it for me."

"What do you write about?"

"I write about being saved. Not by a razor blade, but by love. I guess that's why I like to read, write and draw. I learn a lot, I write excellent short stories and I create great art. Reading about another place that you love or hold dear to your heart is the ultimate escape: I love living someone else's life. Even if it's for twenty chapters, I'm happy."

"Well can't you substitute the cutting for the things you like to do?"

"NO! Cutting is how I cope! I eventually run out of paint, paper, and ink! What the do you think will happen next?" I screamed as I stood up and turned over the table! Not fazed by a damn thing I did, he turned over his tablet and continued to write on his lap.

Pacing the room like a caged animal, my thoughts raced to the finish line. What could I say for this nightmare to end?

"My mind races with thoughts all day long and my mind never asleep. My sleep patterns are off and I want to be alone. Two of my best friends tried to kill themselves and now-they're vegetables. My brother? There is not a day where I don't think of him."

"Meagan, we have a lot of work to do."

"Tell me something I don't know." For some reason, I'm cool on this doctor. He wasn't trying to judge me, he isn't trying to tell me how to live---he's just asking about me about my feelings!

"What else?"

"Tonight, my mother only acted concerned because she caught me. I have not heard her famous, "Come to me speech" since my brother passed! Even though he's no longer here, but she still holds onto him. She never consoled me when he died. I'm still here, I have feelings too."

"Do you think your family is willing to sit down and talk things out at group therapy? Your entire family needs to heal and try to move on.

"I want my family to talk about my brother's death, I want them to go to his grave more, I want to laugh and cry about him anytime, anywhere!"

"It sounds as if your family never grieved at all. It sounds as if they have taken the wrong approach in moving on with life. Meagan, take one day at a time. Cutting yourself is not healthy. You can't escape the grief you are experiencing.

"Okay, I do not disagree with anything you said, but how do I stop hurting myself?"

"This is going to be a lot of work, but you can do it. You asked the right question, which shows you are admitting your problem. I must inform you that through our conversations, self-injury is not your only problem. You are also suffering with depression. I know it's too much to swallow at one time, but take the time to digest what I have said. I recommend that we start you on some medication. To start off, I'd like for you to see me and a therapist once a week."

"That's a lot."

"It's going to take a lot in the beginning but I anticipate you getting better. Can we work together, Meagan?"

"Sure, long as you help my family too. I want them to know that Eric will not be upset if we take family vacations, if we go to the movies together and if we laugh together. We will never forget him."

"You're a bright girl. Please stay for at least three days. Let's get you started on your medication. I want to see how you respond to it. While you're here, please participate in group therapy. It will help more than you think."

"Okay- I'd rather stay anyways. I don't want to see my parents right now."

"Great, let's get started, shall we?"

## Facts about Cutting

Cutting, also called; 'self harm, self- injury, burning, or self-mutilation. It generally occurs mostly amongst teenagers and often times carries into young adulthood. In this act of self-injury, the body obtains deliberate damages, without the visual intention of suicide. This is not failed suicide! This is one of the biggest misunderstandings about 'cutters.'

There are many reasons why teenagers and young adults choose to cut /self mutilate. Here are a few reasons.

- It's a way to deal with pain, strong emotions, heavy pressure, or relationship problems.
- The relief from bad feelings eats away at the individual. They express 9through cutting) feelings of rage, sorrow, rejection, desperation, longing, or emptiness.
- There is a display of poor coping skills. The person cannot adapt to change. New people or situations overwhelm the individual.

- Lack of being able to express themselves.
- Individuals who tend to cut, have been linked to having other psychological problems.

## Warning Signs

- Wearing of long sleeved shirts all the time! The most obvious time is during the summertime.
- Frequent complaining of accidental injuries to one's own self. Cat or dog scratches/bites.
- Avoiding situations for anyone to see their body limbs or areas of infliction.

## Why Cut?

- People who choose this emotional exit, perform cutting to deal with certain feelings of unreality, or numbness. They also do this to try stopping numbness, or to relieve the tension.

## Treatment Options

Most psychiatrists prescribe antidepressants, or mood stabilizers. Next, the patient is taught coping mechanisms to replace the act of self-injury. Upon arrival of stability, the patient's next step is to experience a high level of therapy. From there, they work their way down; until the therapist feels that the patient has made plenty headway.

*Londa B.*

## Final Words

I hope this book provided you the insight to the lives of the mentally ill and their loved ones. I look at my walk in life and there are times I become upset about the things that were done to me physically and mentally. However, the longer I live, I see purpose in life. I pray that through my literature you will be able to find truth, understanding, and peace. If you suspect your loved ones, friends or you suffering from a mental condition…get help! Don't wait, sometimes the outcome can be deadly.

This book is not to be used a medical guide to diagnosing or treating a mental illness. Seek a board certified and licensed psychiatrist.

On a more personal note to my African American family. We seem to be on the top ten list of every type of disease. NOW, we are on the top ten list for mental illnesses! The facts however, SHOULD NOT, startle you. Factor in the socioeconomics and the way in which we treat our bodies and the way we harbor stress

and bad experiences; and you have the perfect
equation for mental health issues.


Take a look at the facts that my friends at
NAMI have gathered (true, factual data) about
African Americans.

- Cultural biased opinions against mental
  health professionals and health care professionals prevent many AA's (African
  Americans) from seeking care due to
  previous experiences. Some which may
  have included misdiagnosis, inadequate
  treatment, and lack of cultural understanding by healthcare professionals.
- AA's tend to rely on family and spiritual
  outlets to help them with their
  health/mental issues.
- In the African American community
  Mental illnesses are frequently stigma-
  tized and misunderstood.
- Most AA's are at a socioeconomic dis-
  advantage in the availability to attaining
  mental health care.
- Mental illness issues are more prevalent
  in the AA community.
- Somatization (the birth of a physical illness related to mental health) occurs at

15% for AA's and only at 9% for Caucasians.

- AA's metabolize medications more slowly than Caucasians. Yet AA's receive higher dosage of psychiatric meds, which can increase medical side effects.
- Social circumstances serve as the indicator for the likelihood of developing a mental illness.

Get it together my sisters and brothers. We cannot avoid to disregard our mental health! To our community leaders and Pastors, please talk with your congregations. Create a disaster plan for your church. Tragedies happen and a lot of times, people find solace at the altar and not in a physician's office. A disaster plan is used to assist members who have experienced life changing experiences. Murders, illnesses, stress and other life issues. Please create one for your church.

Please do this for me. Go to any mental health website and take a confidential evaluation quiz. Enforce that ALL of your family members take one as well. Our children...they need help as well. More African American teens are taking their lives now! Wellness stars with the mind. Focus on your mental health and the rest will follow.

Mind over Matter...you can do it!

Peace and Blessings to you all.

-*Londa B.*

*Londa B.*

Information and statistics in this book were
provided by NAMI.
National Alliance of Mental Illnesses
www.nami.org

Mental illnesses are medical conditions that dis-
rupt a person's thinking, feeling, mood, ability
to relate to others, and daily functioning. Just
like any other medical disorder, mental illnesses are medical conditions. Most of them result
in a diminished capacity for coping with the or-
dinary demands of life.

Serious mental illnesses include major depression, schizophrenia, bipolar disorder, obsessive
compulsive disorder (OCD), panic disorder,
post traumatic stress disorder (PTSD), and bor-
derline personality disorder. The good news
about mental illness is that recovery is possible.

Mental illnesses can affect persons of any age, race, religion, or income. Mental illnesses are not the result of personal weakness, lack of character, or poor upbringing. Mental illnesses are treatable. Most people diagnosed with a serious mental illness can experience relief from their symptoms by actively participating in an individual treatment plan.

In addition to medication treatment, psychosocial treatment such as cognitive behavioral therapy, interpersonal therapy, peer support groups, and other community services can also be components of a treatment plan and that assist with recovery. The availability of transportation, diet, exercise, sleep, friends, and meaningful paid or volunteer activities contribute to overall health and wellness, including mental illness recovery.

Here are some important facts about mental illness and recovery:

- Mental illnesses are biologically based brain disorders. They cannot be overcame through "will power" and are not related to a person's "character" or intelligence.

- Mental disorders fall along a continuum of severity. Even though mental disorders are widespread in the population, the main burden of illness is concentrated in a much smaller proportion — about 6 percent, or 1 in 17 Americans — who suffer from a serious mental illness. It is estimated that mental illness affects 1 in 5 families in America.

- The World Health Organization has reported that four of the 10 leading causes of disability in the US and other developed countries are mental disorders. By 2020, Major Depressive illness will be the leading cause of disability in the world for women and children.

- Mental illnesses usually strike individuals in the prime of their lives, often during adolescence and young adulthood. All ages are susceptible, but the young and the old are especially vulnerable.

- Without treatment the consequences of mental illness for the individual and society are staggering: unnecessary disability, unemployment, substance abuse, homelessness, inappropriate incarceration, suicide and wasted lives; The economic cost of untreated mental illness is more than 100 billion dollars each year in the United States.

- The best treatments for serious mental illnesses today are highly effective; between 70 and 90 percent of individuals have significant reduction of symptoms and improved quality of life with a combination of pharmacological and psychosocial treatments and supports.

- With appropriate effective medication and a wide range of services tailored to their needs, most people who live with serious mental illnesses can significantly reduce the impact of their illness and find a satisfying measure of achievement and independence. A key concept is to develop expertise in developing strategies to manage the illness process.

- Early identification and treatment is of vital importance; By ensuring access to the treatment and recovery supports that are proven effective, recovery is accelerated and the further harm related to the course of illness is minimized.

- Stigma erodes confidence that mental disorders are real, treatable health conditions. We have allowed stigma and a now unwarranted sense of hopelessness to erect attitudinal, structural and financial barriers to effective treatment and recovery. It is time to take these barriers down.

*Londa B.*

## **WEBSITES**

### **HTTP://WWW.LONDAB.COM**

### **NAMI**
## HTTP://WWW.NAMI.ORG

### **NATIONAL MENTAL HEALTH ASSOC.**
## HTTP://WWW.NMHA.COM

### **NATIONAL INSTITUTE OF MENTAL HEALTH**
## HTTP://www.nimh.nih.gov

For more information on cutting, please refer to the website below.

S.A.F.E- Self-Abuse Finally Ends
http://www.selfinjury.com

Or Call

1-800-dontcut

## A Few of my Favorite Quotes

*"Mental Illness is an equal opportunity illness. Every one of us is impacted by mental illness. One in five adults are dealing with this illness, and many are not seeking help because of the stigma prevents that."*
-Margaret Larson

*"Mental health…is not a destination but a process. It's about how you drive, not where you are going."*
-Norman Shpancer, *The Good Psychiatrist*: A Novel

*"Some of the most extraordinary people I have met suffer from mental illness. Their pain forces them to be honest. It doesn't get any realer than that."*
-Helen Perry

*"If people with mental illness can't access the services, it doesn't matter how good those services are. It simply means that we're good in theory only and not in a practical, meaningful way."*
-Dave Almeida

Londa B.